Bagby Street YMCA

Priscilla T Graham

Copyright © 2021 by Priscilla T Graham
All Rights Reserved.
Bagby Street YMCA

ISBN: 978-1-953824-00-4
Printed in the United States of America

All Rights Reserved. No part of this book may be reproduced or transmitted in any form or by any means, electronic or mechanical, including photocopying, recording or any information storage and retrieval system without written permission of the publisher except for brief quotations used in reviews, written specifically for inclusion in a newspaper, blog, or magazine.

Cover design and book layout by Priscilla T Graham

In the making of this book, every attempt has been made to verify names, facts, and figures.

Photos from the Graham Collection, Informer News Paper, Red Book, and Public Domain

Written by Priscilla T Graham

www.priscillatgraham.com

Priscilla Graham Photography & Publishing

*Dedicated to my father, Bobby Graham.
African American History is American History.*

Content

Bagby Street YMCA 1948-1954	6
The Century Club	9
William Craver	19
Work As If It All Depends On You	26
Building Fund Campaign	31
Bagby Street YMCA Day Camp	33
Thirty Fifth	48
YMCA Service Award 1954	55
Groundbreaking	59
Dedication of Camp Holden Sign 1954	62
Cornerstone Laying Ceremony	66
Thirty-Sixth Annual Meeting	68
Building Program Radiothon 1955	79
Dedication Ceremony and Open House	82

Bagby Street 1948-54

Year	Board Chair	Executive Director
1954	Dr. E.B. Perry	Quentin R. Mease
1950-54	Percy Harrison Holden	Quentin R. Mease
1950	Percy Harrison Holden	Quentin R. Mease Interim
1948-49	Percy Harrison Holden	William Curtis Craver

YMCA Thrift Week Observance

The Seventh Annual Thrift Week Observance sponsored by the YMCA and affiliates closed on Sunday, February 2nd with a public Exhibition of boys' posters from over 15 Y Clubs. The first place winner received an all-expense paid session of summer camp. Second and third place winners also received an award. Mr. George S. Nelson President of the local Barber's Association and owner of Nelson's Barbershop was the event speaker.

Annual Southwest Area Council

On March 5-6, delegates from Houston's 7 branches attended the Annual Southwest Area Council YMCA held in Waco, Texas. The Bagby Street YMCA representatives included Chairman P.H. Holden and Executive Secretary William C. Craver. Frank L. Lane and E.S. Harrison were selected as alternates. The council was designed to make policies and laws governing local associations in the area. 15 Negro YMCAs also sent representatives.

Go To Church Sunday

The Hi Y and Gra Y Clubs totaling membership of nearly 2,000 under the leadership of J.C. McDade and A.R. Turner sponsored *Go To Church Sunday* on March 7. The members of the 40 clubs attend church in a body directed by their sponsor. In 1947, 1,000 boys attended 17 different churches for *Go To Church Sunday*.

Rosenwald Fund

The Julius Rosenwald Fund established in 1917 for the wellbeing of mankind ceased operation on June 30, 1948. The fund has invested $22.5 million dollars in rural schools, Negro colleges, fellowships, and various other projects for Negroes and poor whites for over 30 years.

Citywide Membership Drive

The Y Citywide Membership Drive for sustaining members for Houston's seven branches kickoff was held on March 30, 1948 with a rally and get together with all branches. James Ellenwood of Brooklyn, New York and author of *Look At The Y* gave the opening address. The 1948 Citywide Membership Drive was the first time all seven branches simultaneity launched membership

TIMELINE 1948

February 7, 1948
YMCA Thrift Week Observance To Close Sunday With Exhibit

February 28, 1948
Southwest Council Y To Meet In Waco

Y Boys to Sponsor Go To Church Sunday March Seventh

March 20, 1948
YMCA Membership Drive Opens March 30

Rosenwald Fund Ends June 30

April 10, 1948
Three Y Divisions In Heated Contest

May 8, 1948
Houston Y-Teens Attend Eight State Conference

May 15, 1948
YMCA Goes Over The Top In Financial Campaign

Mrs. Harrison Is Slated To Address Mothers and Daughters

May 22, 1948
Y To Hold Co-Ed Outing
The Y held a one-day Teen Camp for Boys and Girls on the banks of Sandy Creek, Spring, Texas on May 30.

June 5, 1948
YMCA Camps To Open June 22

June 26, 1948
YMCA Campers Off For First Session At Spring

YMCA Sponsors Sunday At Camp

campaigns promoted by the metropolitan YMCA Board of Directors of the City of Houston. The top officers in the Bagby Street YMCA Membership Campaign were Associate Chairman Dr. A.R. Reese, Chairman Hobart Taylor, Sr., and Associate Chairman Sidney Hasgett.

The heated competition between the top three Y Divisions pushed the YMCA over the top of its Financial Campaign. The Membership Campaign Victory Dinner was held on Wednesday, May 12th with Hobart Taylor Campaign Chairman presiding. Over 40 workers and special guest attended. Although the Y did not reach its membership goal of 1,000; they did exceed the Y's financial goal of $4,500 by 11.5 percent. Taylor sold sustaining memberships of $100 each to 27 members. Breaking records that have never been achieved by any previous chairman.

Bagby Street Y Expands Program

Executive Secretary William C. Craver hired Quentin Ronald Mease as a Program Secretary in September 1948 to initiate a special expansion program for young men at the Colored Branch YMCA. The program was designed to organize young men in clubs, forums, study groups, and projects of interest with special attention focusing on

college and university students of the city. The Colored Branch YMCA Chairman P.H. Holden announced the special program and that the Directing Secretary Quentin Mease a native of De Moines, Iowa, was already engaged and on the scene studying the situation and making surveys. Mease office was located in room 300 of the Pilgrim Building, 1217 Bagby Street.

Shortly after arriving on his new assignment, Mease convinced his colleagues to change the name of the small three-room Colored Branch YMCA located in the Pilgrim building on Bagby Street to the Bagby Street Branch YMCA.

TIMELINE 1948

September 25, 1948
Prairie View College Y Holds Annual Retreat

October 2, 1948
Bagby Street Y Expands Program

December 11, 1948
Bagby Street Y Ranks High In The Nation, Says Yearbook Statistics

The Century Club

The idea to develop an organization of contributors who would give $100 or more annually to sponsor Y Youth Work was conceived by the Membership Campaign General Chairman Hobart T. Taylor, Sr. in 1948. Taylor's security plan was to set up a fund backed by as many citizens as possible that would give large and sustainable gifts to *back our neighborhood boys of Houston in a large way*. In the 1948 Membership Campaign, 27 men and women gave their support by donating $100 each for the 1948 activities and pledged their support for 1949. As a result, the Century Club was born with 27 inaugural members: Hobart Taylor, Sr., Mrs. Hobart Taylor, W.L.D. Johnson, Jr., J.B. Grigsby, C.A. Dupree, Mrs. C.A. Dupree, Julius White, M.L. Ward, Dr. Lorenzo Kelly, Archie Wells, L.W. Dickerson, Mrs. Ann Robinson, Reverend S.A. Pleasants, Dr. C.L. Barnes, Dr. I.B. Bryant, W.S. Holland, Dr. Lonnie Smith, L.H. Spivey, Carl Barnes, Carter Wesley, Dr. John W. Davis, W.H. Smith, Edward McCullough, Dr. W.J. Minor, Zuber Tire Company, Deats Oil Company, and Burkett Motors.

The Century Club

The Century Club is an association of individual donors and representatives of business firms who believe in the importance of the YMCA's citizenship training program for youth and who support that belief with an annual membership contribution of $100 or more.

A YMCA Century Club Member:

- Believes that youth are his or her community's greatest asset
- Feels a personal responsibility for helping guide young people in the right direction
- Knows that the development of strong leaders of tomorrow require the highest skill that trained leadership can provide today
- Backs his or her interest in the future of the youth with an annual membership contribution of $100 or more to his or her YMCA

As A Century Club Member You Will:

- Help the YMCA meet the challenge of a rapidly growing youth population by enabling it to extend its services
- Bring the benefits of YMCA membership to countless more young people who desire to participate in its activities
- Enable the YMCA to strengthen particularly those phases of its program which combat the evil forces that prey upon teenage youth
- Insure the financial stability of the YMCA

Who May Belong?

- Any citizen or representative of a business firm who endorses the purposes and program of the YMCA and who wishes to advance *Y* work in his or her community by a membership contribution of $100 or more.
- 1963-66 Hobart Taylor, Sr. *Mr. Century Club* lead all campaign workers for three consecutive years and retired the *Chairman's Trophy* for top production.
- Carl Walker, Jr. retired two *Chairman's Trophies* for his Century Club membership production and leadership of Century Club Membership Campaigns production. He was the top individual and team leader in six consecutive years with a total of 236.
- Eddie Young also won the *Chairman's Trophy* for his high production and leadership of Century Club Membership Campaigns.

E.O. Smith Jr. Hi Y and Gra Y with sponsors T.L. Lampley and Albert Barrett and Theodore R. Chatman, Principal

E.O. Smith Junior Hi Y Club members with sponsors Robert Gay, Thornton L. Lampley, Principal T.R. Chatman, Vice Principal Wendell Terrell

Hobart Taylor, Sr.

Mrs. Hobart Taylor, Sr.

L.H. Spivey

Dr. C.L. Barnes

Titus Barnes
Carl Barnes Funeral Home

Dr. W.J. Minor

W.S. Holland

Carter Wesley

Dr. Lonnie Smith

C.A. Dupree

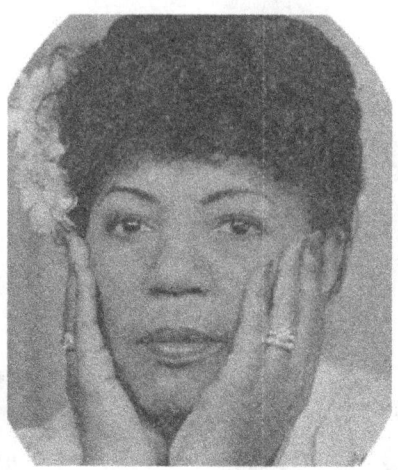
Mrs. C.A. Dupree

W.L.D. Johnson, Jr.

J.B. Grigsby
Julius White
M.L. Ward
Dr. Lorenzo Kelly
L.W. Dickerson
W.H. Smith
Zuber Tire Company

Reverend S.A. Pleasants
Dr. I.B. Bryant
Archie Wells
Dr. John W. Davis
Edward McCullough
Deats Oil Company
Burkett Motors

Mrs. Ann Robinson

Dr. J.T. Sprott with Hi Y Student

YMCA Business Week

YMCA Business Week Trainee

Dr. J.T. Sprott with Master Orville Dean

M.W. McDonald Physical Education Committee Chairman presents trophies to youth members

Johnathon Roach, Sponsor and Youth Church participants

Hi Y Conference at Prairie View University

H.M. Washington presents trophy to sponsor, David Bradford's Phillis Wheatley Hi Y Club

Annual Membership Meeting

The Bagby Street YMCA held its 18th Annual Membership Meeting on Thursday, March 29, 1949. Over one hundred men and women volunteered as campaign workers for the branch's largest membership drive *Back Your Neighborhood Boys* to recruit 2,000 boy and men members by April 15, 1949.

The drive was the preliminary launch of a citywide financial campaign approved by the Y Board of Directors and voted on by the Bagby Street Y Board of Management to revive the 1939 Building Campaign to raise funds for a new adequate Negro YMCA building at the corner of Gray and Hutchins. General Chairman, W.L.D. Johnson, Jr. stated that the Bagby Street YMCA 1939 Building Program was haunted by the outbreak of World War II. Negroes were asked to raise $50,000; however, were only able to collect $33,000 of the $60,000 pledged. As a result, to ensure the new campaigns success, both white and Negro citizens united in 1949 to raise monies and design plans for an adequate YMCA facility.

1949 Accomplishments

1) Membership 3,500
2) Underprivileged boys served through game room, camp and clubs 300
3) 44 Y Clubs for boys and young men throughout the city in schools and neighborhoods
4) Father and son programs helped and served 4,000 fathers and sons during March 1949
5) Over 800 fathers and sons attended the Annual Fellowship Meet

Father and Son Observance Week

The Bagby Street YMCA began its 17th Annual Father and Son Observance Week on February 27. Thirty eight Hi Y and Gra Y Clubs totaling membership of more than 1,500 boys carried out the big program by visiting the 30 cooperating churches for *Go To Church Sunday*. During the week, the boys and fathers attended celebration meetings, discussion groups, and parties in honor of fathers and sons. As a program climax, a big fellowship meeting of fathers and sons was held on Friday March 4 at 8:00 pm in Phyllis Wheatley High School gym.

TIMELINE 1949

January 8, 1949
Bagby Street YMCA Has A Eventful Year In 1948

Bagby Street YMCA Plans Large Summer Program

February 26, 1949
The Bagby Street YMCA Begins 17th Annual Father and Son Observance Week

Theo Harris Elected 2nd Vice President of YMCA Committee

March 19, 1949
YMCA Stars Upset Bee Bee Tabernacle

Bagby Street YMCA Holds Membership Kick Off Meet Tuesday Nite

March 29, 1949
YMCA Membership Drive Has Kickoff Tuesday

April 23, 1949
Bagby Street YMCA Extend Services To Young Men

Bagby Street Y Membership Roundup Extended

YMCA Track Meet Saturday

July 2, 1949
YMCA First Balloting Election Novel Affair

Real Democracy Is Needed Says Mrs. E Roosevelt

July 9, 1949
YMCA Camps In Season At Spring, Texas

Bagby Street YMCA To Close 32nd Camping Session

Theo Harris Second Vice President

The 1949 Southwest Area of the National Council YMCA consisting of 75 associations including 13 branches serving Negro boys and men was held in Fort Worth, Texas.

One hundred and twelve delegates from Arkansas, Oklahoma, and Texas were in attendance including 16 Negro delegates.

During the closing session, Theo Harris was elected Second Vice President for the ensuing year. This was the first time a Negro was elected by the Southwest Area of the National Council YMCA to serve in a presidential capacity.

Harris Sales Executive of Atlanta Life Insurance Company served as a member of the Bagby Street YMCA Board of Management, World Service Chairman, and branch Assistant Recording Secretary. Also attending the council meeting was Daniel Gray and Executive Secretary William C. Craver.

First Balloting Election

The Bagby Street YMCA held its first election under new bylaws with the membership casting ballots in the election of members of the Board of Management. There were 26 candidates running for 18 offices.

TIMELINE 1949

August 6, 1949
YMCA Camp Closes A Very Successful Year

August 18, 1949
Nadine Craver, Dexter L. Thomas Was In A Beautiful Home Ceremony Here

September 17, 1949
YMCA Staff Members Attend Area Meeting

September 24, 1949
Bagby Branch YMCA Offering Class In Public Speaking

December 10, 1949
Booker T. Washington Jr. Y Teens Visit Phenix Dairy

December 17, 1949
YMCA Hoop Managers To Meet

Langston Elementary Football Team with Principal George R. Munline on right and Y member on the left

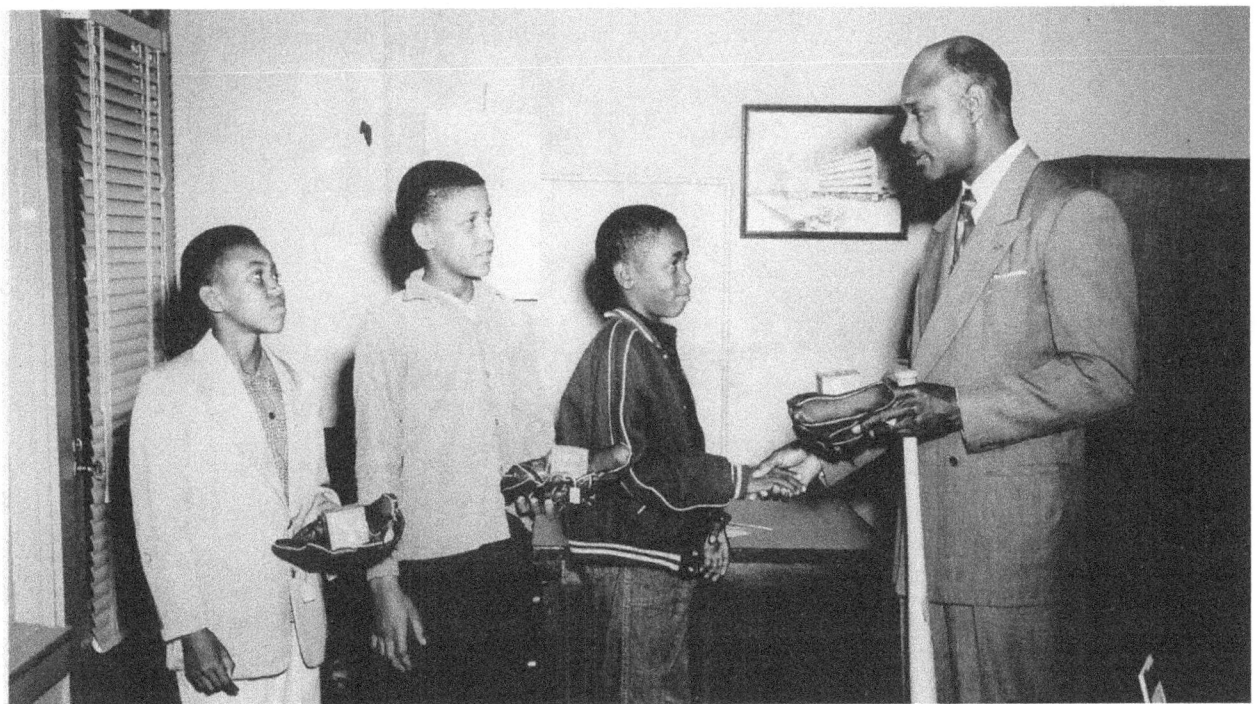
Youth members receive bats and balls from W.G. Strain, Board Member

Membership Campaign Workers
Mrs. Helen D. Brooks and Daniel Gay

Boys Secretary Thornton Lampley presents trophy to Mrs. Lorene Lancelin

William Craver

During his 18-year tenure in Houston, Craver established a lay committee of 150 volunteer men supervising 15 divisions of work representing every section of the city and every section of society.

The 15 divisions included the following: work for boys, service for industrial workers, a more widespread religious work, enlarged education and publicity, physical division, a program for foreign work, financial section, and interracial work for the city and state, a more comprehensive and united effort among the churches, a social and headquarters committee, a committee on leadership personnel and permanent membership organization. Craver also setup Junior College student associations aimed at developing the students' all-around leadership skills.

The committee of management under the leadership of Dr. F.F. Stone elected the following 1931 committee members to head up these various divisions:

Religious Work	Reverend J.I. Donaldson
Interracial	Professor J.D. Ryan
Educational	Dr. W.J. Howard and Professor R.M. Catchings
Physical	Professor J.E. Codwell
Interchurch	Professor E.O. Smith
Boys Work	Professor R.G. Lockett
Industrial	Miles W. Jordan and P.C. Colvin
Membership	H.P. Carter and G.H. Webster
Social and House	H.E. McCoy
Finance	O.J. Polk associated with E.O. Smith and J.W. Hubert

The General Director of Membership Howard Payne Carter along with five major directors that presided over the workers in the Wards.

The Ward Directors

Third Ward	Dr. I.K. Darby
Fifth Ward	C.C. Penn
Second Ward	Ray Williams
Fourth Ward	Walter Hurd
First and Sixth Ward	Dr. R.H.

Each director had a number of captain directors who lead various groups of his Ward.

The branch established its own summer camp, Camp Mays at Spring, Texas serving over 641 boys annually. Craver increased the branch's membership to over 4,025 members and established 40 clubs. Under his leadership, the YMCA established the Annual Father and Son Banquet, Julius Rosenwald Interracial Relationships Program, Our Men and Missions Day in the World of Service attracting from 400 to 700 men annually since 1932.

Executive Secretary William Craver increased the YMCA's professional staff from one to five and expanded its services throughout the city of Houston. He hired Quentin Ronald Mease as a Program Secretary in September 1948 to initiate a special expansion program for young men at the Bagby Street YMCA. The program was designed to organize young men in clubs, forums, study groups, and projects of interest with special attention focusing on college and university students of the city. The Bagby Street YMCA Chairman P.H. Holden announced the special program and that the Directing Secretary Quentin Mease a native of De Moines, Iowa, was already engaged and on the scene studying the situation and making surveys. Mease office was located in room 300 of the Pilgrim Building, 1217 Bagby Street.

William Craver's labors and achievements through the years have been far beyond the call of duty. He has rendered immeasurable services not only to his people in Houston but to the entire Southwest. Robert J. Maloney

William C. Craver's Retirement Celebration
P.H. Holden, Bagby Street Branch YMCA Board Chairman congratulates William C. Holden on his retirement (January 1950).

Quentin R. Mease, Interim Secretary, William C. Craver, and Thornton Lampley Boys Secretary (January 1950 Craver's Retirement)

William Craver Leaves the YMCA After 30 Years

William Craver sacrificed bright opportunities in law, business, and medicine to dedicate his life to the YMCA. After thirty years of service, Craver retired January 1950. The Testimonial Dinner given in his honor was held at Antioch Baptist Church on January 20, 1950.

On January 11, 1950, Robert J. Maloney, General Secretary of Houston Metropolitan Association stated that *William Craver's labor and achievements through the years have been far beyond the call of duty. He has rendered immeasurable services not only to his people in Houston but the entire Southwest.*

W. C. Craver To Retire As 'Y' Leader After 30 Years; Mease Named

Resigning Secretary
W. C. CRAVER

New "Y" Executive
Q. R. MEASE

HOUSTON — William Curtis Craver will retire as executive secretary of the Bagby tSreet Y.M.C.A. this month after 30 years service with the association, 18 of them in Houston.

P. H. Holden, chairman of the branch committee of management, has appointed Quentin R. Mease as acting executive until his committee has selected a permanent successor. Mr. Mease, a graduate

(See CRAVER, P. 8)

Chairman P.H. Holden appointed Mease in January 1950 as interim Executive Secretary of the Bagby Street Y.

Work As If It All Depends On You
Play As If It All Depends On God

The Bagby Street YMCA held its Annual Meeting on Wednesday, March 14, 1951. The Annual Meeting was presided over by J.W. Robinson, Sr, Chairman of the Annual Meeting Committee. The invocation was given by Reverend A.W. Harley, Jr. Director of New Projects Methodist Churches. Blackshear Instrumental Group and Blackshear All Boys Choir provided the musical entertainment. Miss Goldine Penn performed a solo selection. Nathaniel Shackelford, Dorie Miller Gra Y Club and Paul Nickerson, Booker T. Washington Hi Y Club gave brief presentations on *The Y and I…*

Dr. J.E. Codwell, Chairman presented the Nominating Committee's Report and P.H. Holden, Chairman Board of Management gave the Chairman's Report.

Dr. J.S. Scott, President Wiley College was the principle speaker. Recognition was given by Robert J. Maloney, General Secretary, Young Men's Christian Association.

1950 was a trying year for the Bagby Street YMCA. The pressures of expanding programs under inadequate facilities and a staff in transition created undue hardship on both staff and volunteers resulting in the Y adopting priorities in programming with an emphasis on boy's work and community programming.

Despite severe budget stringencies, membership and program activities soared to new heights. Registered members reached an all-time high, 4,554. Branch sponsored activities also established new records. The inauguration of a full scale summer recreation program in Houston Proper and outlying areas was extremely successful. The branch developed new activities to serve the growing needs of adults and young adults. Established programs such as Hi Y, Gra Y, Neighborhood Clubs, boy's and young men's athletic teams and leagues, summer camping, religious training groups, Older Boy's Conferences and training institutes all continued to flourish.

1950 marked the close of thirty one years of service of the Bagby Street YMCA (Colored YMCA) to the Houston Negro community despite inadequate facilities and equipment the Y has pressed onward and forward.

It Happened At Bagby In 1950

172	different organized groups participated in branch programs
62	Hi Y, Gra Y, and N Y Club groups functioned during the year
4,552	registered YMCA members-all time branch record
436	attended annual Father Son Fellowship Meet (March 1950)
142	volunteers worked in 1950 membership campaign
2,618	different persons were registered for the summer program
71	different persons given swim lessons
1,168	personal interviews and conferences by staff and volunteer personnel

$700	contribution made to permanent camp fund by Mr. and Mrs. Robert A. Childers
4	outpost neighborhood centers established at Acreage Homes, Sunnyside, West End, and Kelly Courts
24	adults registered in first Dale Carnegie speech course of which 16 graduated
73	boys and young men attended out of town training conferences
$214	contributed by boy's clubs to YMCA World Services Fund
27	outside groups used branch facilities during the year
173	volunteers awarded Leaders' Fellowship Cards for lay service at November Fall Conference
13,389	game room usage individual services

Group Activities

Activity	# of Groups	Enrollment	#Sessions	Attendance
Clubs	62	1,076	596	26,040
Classes	3	61	43	872
Teams	38	464	112	2,418
Committee, Boards, Councils	21	177	31	328
Special Events Social	11		11	861
Special Events Athletic	4		4	1,146
Informal Play Groups	17		33	12,552
Trips-Outings	16		16	411

Income

Membership	$5,521.75	24.3%
Program Services	532.02	2.3%
Business	542.33	2.4%
Contributions	$15,980.00	71.0%
Total Income	$22,576.10	100%

Expenses

Program	$4,956.60	22.0%
Business	612.32	2.7%
General Administrative	$14,931.09	66.3%
Building Maintenance	2,020.96	9.0%
Total Income	$22,521.17	100%
1950 Gain	$ 54.93	

Board of Directors

President	George A. Butler
Vice President	E.E. Townes
Vice President	R.A. Farnsworth
Vice President	E.J. Mosher
Recording Secretary	J.O. Webb
Treasurer	J.E. Anderson
General Secretary	Robert J. Maloney

Rex G. Baker	W. Browne Baker	Warren S. Bellows
Jewel A. Benson	Joel H. Berry	E.A. Blackburn
J.E. Burkhart	Robert A. Childers	E.A. Craft
J.H. Crooker, Jr.	W.A. Crute	Lewis W. Cutrer
James G. Donovan	R.D. Ernst	E.R. Filley
Lamar Fleming, Jr.	Ed E. Hall	A.S. Moody, Jr.
Ralph Neuhaus	H.M. Seydler	R.E. Smith
Howard Tellepsen	Tom Tellepsen	Gavin Ulmer
J.H. Wimberly		

Board of Management

Chairman	P.H. Holden
Vice Chairman	Dr. E.B. Berry
Recording Secretary	Theo Harris

Henry J. Bolding, Jr.	J.M. Calhoun	J.E. Codwell
J.R. Cunningham	Dr. J.W. Davis	C.A. Dupree
Daniel Gay	J.H. Jemison	W.L.D. Johnson, Jr.
W.P. Jordan	R.O. Lanier	L.J. Mann
Arthur McCullough, Jr.	J.C. McDade	W.J. Nelson
J.W. Robinson	Hobart Taylor, Sr.	William Sweeny

Branch Staff

Executive Secretary	Quentin R. Mease
Boy's Secretary	Lawrence G. Sims
Physical Director	James F. Brooks
Assistant Boy's Work	James A. Walls
Assistant Boy's Work	Jonathan Roach
Assistant Boy's Work	Hamah R. King
Office Secretary	Bertha L. Johnson

Bagby Street Branch Committees At Work

• Dr. John E. Codwell, Chairman	Board Nominating Committee
o Daniel Gay and L.J. Mann	Members
• Judson Robinson, Sr., Chairman	Annual Meeting Committee
o J.R. Cunningham, WP Jordan, and William Sweeny	Members
• J.C. McDade, Chairman	Boy's Work
• Dr. J.E. Codwell, Chairman	Physical Work
• J.R. Cunningham, Chairman	Camp
• Daniel Gay, Chairman	Men's Membership
• Arthur McCullough, Jr., Chairman	Boy's Membership
• Dr. John W. Davis, Judson W. Robinson, Sr., Co Chairmen	Finance
• C.A. Dupree, Chairman	Building Planning
• P.H. Holden, Chairman	Executive Committee
• W.L.D. Johnson, Jr., Chairman	World Service
• J.H. Jemison, Chairman	Adult Program
• Theo Harris, Chairman	Interracial Intercultural

1951 Goals of New 5 Year Program

- Complete New Building Campaign
- Dedicate site of New Building
- Staff training program for New Building
- Select new site for Boy's Camp
- Development of Young Adult Program
- Improvement of Community Extension Services
- Expansion of Summer Recreation Program
- Development of new lay leadership
- Promotion of successful membership campaign

Business and Professional Men's Club dinner guests, Chief Morrison, Caption Seber, Lt. Spradley, on May 30, 1951.

Bagby Street YMCA Day Camp

Building Fund Campaign

Following years of building good will and successful fundraising efforts, the long-awaited building campaign for the Bagby Street YMCA was launched in 1952. The Houston Metropolitan YMCA launched a $2.5 Million City Wide Building Fund Campaign to build 5 new Ys in the Houston area and plans to purchase additional land and equipment for Camp Wimberly. Bagby Street YMCA was top priority for an $800,000 modern six story building and an additional $65,000 allotment for the acquisition of a 60-acre wooded site in northwest Houston for a year-round camp for the Bagby Street YMCA in plans released in a joint statement on March 27, 1952 by Edward J. Mosher, President of the Houston Young Men's Christian Association, and P. H. Holden, Chairman of the Board of Management of the Bagby Street Branch YMCA.

The additional allotment of $65,000 for the recently acquired Bagby Street YMCA Camp was included in the citywide goal. Furnishings and equipment for the building and camp increased the total cost of the two Bagby Street YMCA projects to over the $900,000 mark. Mr. Mosher, President of the Mosher Steel Company, served as general chairman of the big drive, which was held during the month of May.

Prominent Houston attorney and business executive George A. Butler was head of the campaign steering committee. At the time the building plans were initiated, Butler was President of the YMCA. Members of the Bagby Street Branch steering committee who worked with the metropolitan group on plans for the new building for more than a year were P.H. Holden, Dr. John W. Davis, J. M. Calhoun, C. A. Dupree, Daniel Gay, J. H. Jemison, L. J. Mann, Arthur McCullough Jr., J. C. McDade, Dr. E. B. Perry, Judson W. Robinson, and Hobart T. Taylor.

Six Story Structure Building Design

The new Bagby Street building will be of the most modern contemporary design, embodying: the regional style of architecture so prevalent in this section of the United States and Latin America.

A Six Story structure with foundation support for two additional floors in the future, the building will contain the most advanced features to be found in association buildings erected in recent years.

Equipped with the latest type elevators, the building will contain both adult and youth lounges; a number of all-purpose club rooms, food service facilities; a complete physical department including gymnasium, swimming pool, and a large residence section.

The T shaped design of the proposed structure will provide not only provisions for two additional floors, but another wing may be added to the residence section, thereby doubling the capacity of room accommodations.

The new Bagby Street YMCA Camp was located on West Montgomery Road, one mile north of FM 1960 and twenty-four miles from downtown. The fifty-five acres camping site included a large new 210 feet air conditioned and centrally heated ranch house, a six-room cottage, a large outdoor swimming pool, and a 15-acre lake facility. The appraised valuation of the property formerly owned by a Texas oil millionaire was $140,000.

During the summer, this beautifully wooded area was the ideal vacation spot for over six hundred boys and adult groups throughout the year.

Two campers fishing at Camp Holden with Physical Director, James F. Brooks

Campers at Camp Holden

Campers watch Camp Director James A. Walls about to dive into the pool at Camp Holden.

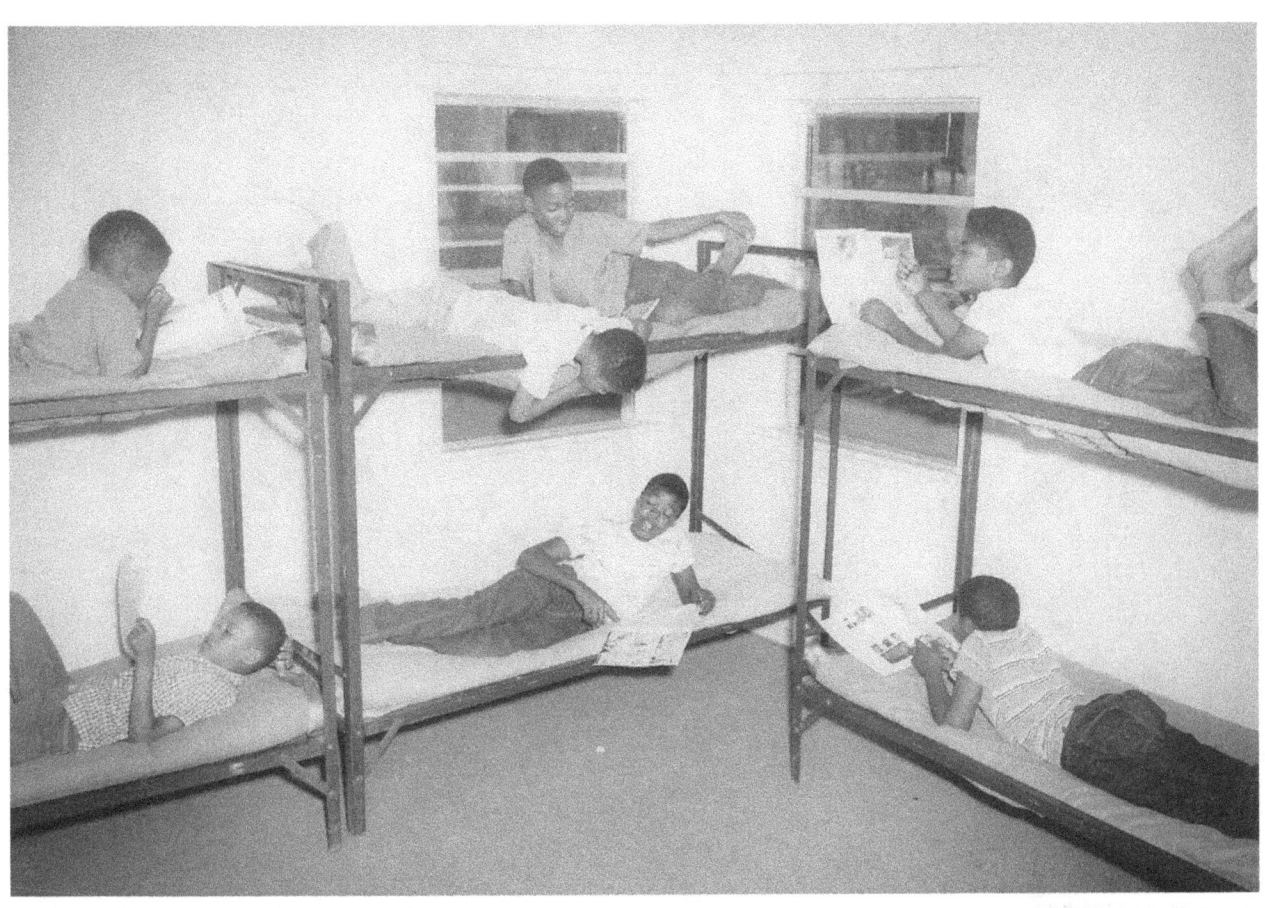

Mrs. Dirk D. Peters, Housemother, Nicholson, and Theodore Stewart severing lunch to campers

Building Campaign

Building Program Committee: Dr. Chase W. Pemberton, E.R. Harris, L.H. Spivey, Emerson C. Norris, W.L.D. Johnson and James W. White

Industrial Team

Team Captains of the Industrial division preparing reports for Chairman Daniel Gay Standing J.H. Jemison, Chairman of the Building Fund Campaign on right Daniel Gay, W.G. Stain, and James M. Calhoun

Special Gifts
Special Gifts and Young Men's Teams
Conrad Johnson, L.H. Spivey, James T. Dean, and E.R. Moore at Special Gifts Table

Camp
J.R. Cunningham standing and members of the Camp Team shown reporting during the 1952 drive

Arthur Harding, Building Campaign, addressing board and staff members

Dr. Pemberton addressing campaign volunteers

Camp Committee Members
J.C. McDade, James Cunningham, Lawrence G. Sims, and Youth Work Director

Building Campaign workers Clifton W. Smith, C.A. Dupree, A.G. Hardy, A.E. Warner, and Juduis Carter

Arthur Harding Campaign Director congratulates Gus T. Harris, Jack Yates High School Instructor on his fine report

J.H. Jemison receives check from Beauticians for the YMCA Building Fund

On Thursday, December 24, 1953, the completion of the new Bagby Street YMCA building architectural plans on Wheeler Avenue at Sampson Street was announced in a joint meeting by P.H. Holden, Chairman of the Board of Management, and J.H. Jemison, Chairman of the Building Program Committee.

The plans were considerably revised after Lamar Fleming donated three acres of land for a new site for the Y structure on April 29, 1953. The original plans were drawn up in 1952 for the site on Gray and Hutchins; however, to make more practical use of the additional land afforded by the new site the new design and layout of the building provided an additional 8,000 square feet of floor space.

The modernistic three story and basement building will face 200 feet along Wheeler Avenue and extended back 290 feet on Sampson Street. The foundation will be constructed as to permit the addition of two additional stories to the front section of the building in the future.

The new edifice has been laid out in three main sections. The three story front section and basement will house the administrative, residential, and business features of the plant; the program section located in the center will contain club rooms, craft shops, and the food service department. A patio separates the two front units and the third section which comprises the natatorium and gymnasium at the rear.

Some of the outstanding features of the new building and site which will cost one million dollars will be the residence section containing seventy furnished rooms, separate youth and adult programs facilities consisting of lounges, club rooms, game rooms and craft shops; coffee shop and banquet room with kitchen facilities to serve each; a large regulation college sized gymnasium, and completely titled swimming pool with a spectator's balcony.

Contract Signing

Louis A. Fisher, President of Fisher Construction Company watches as Edward J. Mosher, President of Houston YMCA sign the contract to start construction of the Bagby Street Branch YMCA Building. J.H. Jemison (standing) Chairman of the branch Building Program Committee, also witnessed the transaction.

Thirty Fifth
BAGBY STREET BRANCH
Young Men's Christian Association
Houston, Texas
January 29, 1954

1953 will, with significant predominance, reflect in *Y* history as being one of our greatest efforts, Harmony, vision, patience, tolerance, and unselfish participation have permeated all activities, from Gra Y clubs to the Board of Management itself.

We take inventory of our work during the past year, realizing as it were, that we are now at the crossroads. For many years, we have continued to expand in spite of inadequate physical facilities. This has been due to the fine, cooperative spirit manifested by the membership, board, and staff alike.

Our program still emphasizes the Christian principles which should govern our everyday living. Our theme has been: how can we best project the objectives of the Young Men's Christian Association in our Democracy? We have gradually, yet with altruistic persistence, obtained recognition and membership on several of the important Metropolitan committees.

We point with pride to our 1953 membership campaign - the largest numerical and financial effort in branch history - proving again that our citizens will always support a worthwhile program. Our recreational program has reached new records; in reaching our membership, our youth clubs have functioned most effectively with suitable increases in all areas. Our new camp, with continuing physical improvements, has given to thousands a much needed facility for relaxation, study and meditation without the distractions of the city.

We are grateful to the citizens of Houston and our Staff who made possible the achievements of last year. And we beg of you, as we see in marvelous, mental silhouette against the horizon - our new building - to stay on the job. We have just begun the long-range program so vital for the youth of our community. Please be assured that bequests, endowment funds, and memorial gifts will greatly strengthen the work of this Association.

Sincerely,
Dr. E.B. Perry
Vice Chairman
Board of Management

The Houston Young Men's Christian Association
Board of Directors

Officers
President	Edward J. Mosher
Vice President	Howard T. Tellepsen
Vice President	R.A. Farnsworth
Vice President	R.A. Childers
Recording Secretary	J.O. Webb
Treasurer	J.E. Anderson
General Secretary	Robert Maloney

Board of Management

Chairman	P.H. Holden
Vice Chairman	Dr. E.B. Berry
Recording Secretary	Theo Harris
Henry J. Bolding, Jr.	Dr. John E. Codwell
C.A. Dupree	J.H. Jemison
Dr. R.O. Lanier	J.C. McDade
Emerson O. Norris	L.H. Spivey
Hobart T. Taylor	Dr. Jonel L. Brown
J.R. Cunningham	P.E. Gallagher
W.L.D. Johnson, Jr.	L.J. Mann
Dr. C.W. Pemberton	W.G. Strain, Jr.
Archie Wells	J.M. Calhoun
Dr. John W. Davis	Daniel Gay
W.P. Jordan	Arthur McCullough, Jr.
W.J. Nelson	Judson W. Robinson
William Sweeney	James W. White

Staff

Executive Secretary	Quentin R. Mease
Boys' Work Secretary	Lawrence G. Sims
Physical Director	James F. Brooks
Camp & Boys' Work	James A. Walls
Assistant Boys' Work	Hayden I. Walker
Assistant Boys' Work	James E. Bryant
Office Secretary	Bertha L. Johnson

Annual Meeting Committee

L.J. Mann, Chairman	Mrs. Vestophia Gunnells
Emerson G. Norris	Mrs. Estella Higgins
W.P. Jordan	Mrs. Martha McAfee
H.M. Washington	

Bagby Branch Committees

Boys' Work	J.C. McDade, Chairman
Physical Work	Emerson C. Norris, Chairman
Camp	J.C. Cunningham, Chairman
Men's Membership	Daniel Gay, Chairman
Boys' Membership	Arthur McCullough, Jr., Chairman
Finance	Dr. John W. Davis, Chairman
Adult Program	James W. White, Chairman
Building Program	J.H. Jemison, Chairman
World Services	W.G. Strain, Sr., Chairman
Interracial Intercultural	Dr. Jonel L. Brown

It Happened At Bagby In 1953

137	different organized groups participated in branch programs
62	Hi Y, Gra Y, and N Y club groups functioned during the years
5,304	registered YMCA members-an all time branch record
154	volunteers worked in 1953 membership campaign
2,114	different persons participated in 1953 summer program
1,024	personal interviews by staff and volunteer personnel
60	acre tract of farmland in Waller County, Texas given to branch by Dr. and Mrs. W.E. Taylor in November
600	attended annual Father and Son Banquet in March
4	outpost neighborhood centers established at Acreage Homes, Trinity Gardens, Sunnyside, and Kelly Courts
126	boys and young men attended out of town training conferences
$665	contributed by boys' club to YMCA World Service Fund
49	outside organizations used branch facilities during year
$5,000	spent for improvements at Bagby Y Camp during current year
45	laymen and secretaries attended first Fall Conference at Bagby Y Camp in October

Annual Meeting and Service Award
Left to right: Mr. and Mrs. L.J. Mann, Dr. and Mrs. E.B. Perry, Robert J. Maloney, Reverend and Mrs. Earl R. Boone at Annual Meeting and Service Award January 29, 1954

Dr. R.O. Lanier at mike, left to right: Mr. and Mrs. E.C. Norris, Mr. and Mrs., Mr. and --------
Mrs. L.J. Mann at Annual Meeting and Service Award January 29, 1954

PROGRAM
Emerson C. Norris, Toastmaster

Opening Statement	L.J. Mann, Chairman Annual Meeting Committee
The Invocation	Reverend E.R. Boone, Pastor Antioch Baptist Church
Dinner-	
Vocal Selections	Johnny Nash
Report of Nominating Committee	J. C. McDade, Chairman
Election, Board Management	
Resolution	James W. White, Member Board Nominating Committee
Introduction of Guest Speaker	Dr. R. O'Hara Lanier, President Texas Southern University
Address	Dr. J.R. Otis, President Alcorn A&M College
Recognitions	F.L. Lane, Former Chairman Board of Management
	Dr. J.R. Otis, President
Tribute	Ben S. McMillian, Principal Burrus Junior High School
Remarks	Edward J. Mosher, President Board of Directors
Benediction	Reverend L.B. Felder, Pastor Trinity East Methodist Church

Bagby Street Branch Activities
Statistical Summary

Group Activities	Enrollment	No. Groups	Sessions	Attendance
Clubs	1,172	62	762	28,626
Classes	61	3	57	1,172
Teams	521	34	134	3,218
Spec Int Groups	82	4	47	1,429
Councils & Committees	181	23	83	1,647
Other	118	2	31	973

GROUPS WITHOUT DEFINITE

Special Events		14		2,531
Informal Groups		19	47	11,477

Individual Services
Personal Interview				1,024
Game Room Usage				12,411

OUTSIDE GROUPS USING YMCA FACILITIES	Number	Attendance
	49	5,121

Sources of Income

Memberships	$ 8,327.75	
Program Services	4,625.04	
United Fund	17,500.00	
Total Income		$30,452.79

Expenses

Administration	$21,599.69	
Programs	6,786.06	
Building and Maintenance	3,617.41	
Total Expenditures		$30,780.97
Net Accumulated Deficit		$ 328.18

Chairman P.H. Holden Service Award 1954

Curtis Davis presents certificate to P.H. Holden and J.C. McDade presents the trophy 1954

YMCA Service Award 1954
BAGBY STREET BRANCH
Young Men's Christian Association
Houston, Texas
January 29, 1954

Let each man think himself an act of God,
His mind a thought, his life a breath of God;
And let each try, by great thoughts and good deeds,
To show the most of Heaven he hath in him.
 -Phillip James Bailey

P. H. Holden belongs to that select circle of men, anyone of whom might be called, *Mr. YMCA*. So close and long has been his identification with the Young Men's Christian Association, that his name almost immediately comes to mind when the Bagby Street YMCA is mentioned.

A noted educator, high churchman, and successful businessman, *P. H.* has consistently lent his many talents to the development of the work and services of the YMCA, locally, nationally, and internationally. His service on boards, committees, and councils attest to the valuable contribution he has made, through the years, to the Association.

His affiliation and record with the local branch stems from its beginning 35 years ago. But his great genius for organization was not discovered until 1939, when he became general chairman of the first Building Fund Campaign. So great was the success of that drive, under his leadership, that he was elected branch chairman in 1941, serving in that capacity until the present time.

His name and deeds have given added distinction and new meaning to the chairmanship of his board. He has *led-out* in all fund raising efforts of the branch, climaxed by his generous contribution to the 1952 Building Fund Campaign, which topped all gifts secured during this drive.

No man has given as generously and as sacrificially of their time, ability and money, to the building of the Bagby Street YMCA, as P. H. Holden. Of him, it can truly be said:

An Institution Is the Lengthened Shadow of One Man

To Develop Christian Personality

A Mississippi boy who, with pluck and perseverance, scaled the heights of his chosen profession to become a renowned educator, Principal of a leading educational institution in his adopted State of Texas, and to win recognition as an outstanding civic leader in the South's Largest City, best characteristics the epochal life of P. H. Holden.

Born August 20, 1882, on a farm near Vicksburg, Mississippi, one of eight children, young Holden struggled to obtain an elementary and high school education. This persistence was rewarded by his graduating as an honor student and class valedictorian from Alcorn A&M College in l905.

A long and lustrous teaching career was begun that same year in Waller County, Texas. In 1907, he accepted a position with the Houston Public Schools, in which system he remained for 45 years. Serving with distinction of various levels, Professor Holden terminated his extended career on educator upon his retirement in 1951 after 26 years as Principal of Burrus Junior High School.

His religious, civic and business activities include membership in Trinity East Methodist Church, of which he is a Trustee, Church Treasurer, and Chairman of the Financial Committee: a Life Member of National Education Association and, also, a Life Member of the Texas State Teachers' Association; and many other affiliations too numerous to mention. P.H. Holden was cited as *Houston's Most Valuable Citizen* in 1941.

Victory Handshake 1952 Building Campaign

General Secretary Robert J. Maloney congratulates J.H. Jemison and P.H. Holden at the end of the 1952 Building Program Campaign

L.H. Spivey and Dr. Eugene B. Perry Bagby Street Branch YMCA Board Chairman

Dr. Eugene B. Perry Bagby Street Branch YMCA Board Chairman and Robert J. Maloney, General Secretary

Camp Committee Members
Left to right: Harold Clark, J.C. McDade, Chairman, Mrs. Estella Higgins, James Cunningham, Mrs. Ella M. Smith, W.G. Strain, and YMCA Staff Member

Camp Committee Members
Standing left to right: A.E. Warner, J.C. McDade, Elbert R. Curvey, C.A. Reissland, Arthur M. Gaines, Jr., and Thornton Lampley

Seated from left to right: Mrs. Estella Higgins, Mrs. Ella M. Smith, James Cunningham, Chairman (center), Mrs. Naomi S. White, and Mrs. Martha McDade

Groundbreaking for the Bagby Street YMCA Building
President of the Houston YMCA Edward J. Mosher, Mary Holden, Hi Y Club Member Wilbur Holmes, Principal Benefactor Lamar Fleming, Jr., and Dr. E.B. Perry

Realization A Long Sought Dream
In 1954, the realization of a long sought dream came to fruition with the ground breaking for the site of the Bagby Street Branch YMCA to be built on 26 lots of land on Wheeler Avenue, some three acres of land located two blocks from Texas Southern University, donated on April 29, 1953 by Lamar Fleming, Jr.

Lamar Fleming, Jr., donor of the building site, breaks first ground for the Bagby Street Branch YMCA Building

Dr. E.B. Perry and Edward Mosher groundbreaking for the Bagby Street Branch YMCA Building

Edward J. Mosher, President of Houston YMCA

Hi Y Club Member Wilbur Holmes groundbreaking for the Bagby Street Branch YMCA Building

Dedication of Camp Holden Sign 1954

James R. Cunningham and Frank Lane　　　　James R. Cunningham, Frank L. Lane, Elbert R. Curry, Clayton Shephard, W.G. Strain

Sam and Emma Taylor

William C. Craver speaks at camp dedication at Camp Holden August 29, 1954

Mrs. Mary Holden widow of the late P.H. Holden receives the portrait of her husband from Ben S. McMillian, Principal, Burrus Junior High School, donor of the portrait

Dr. Charles W. Pemberton addresses members at Camp Holden on left Arthur M. Gaines, Jr. and Henry J. Bolding

Construction of the Bagby Street Branch YMCA

Gra Y Youth Members view cornerstone placement

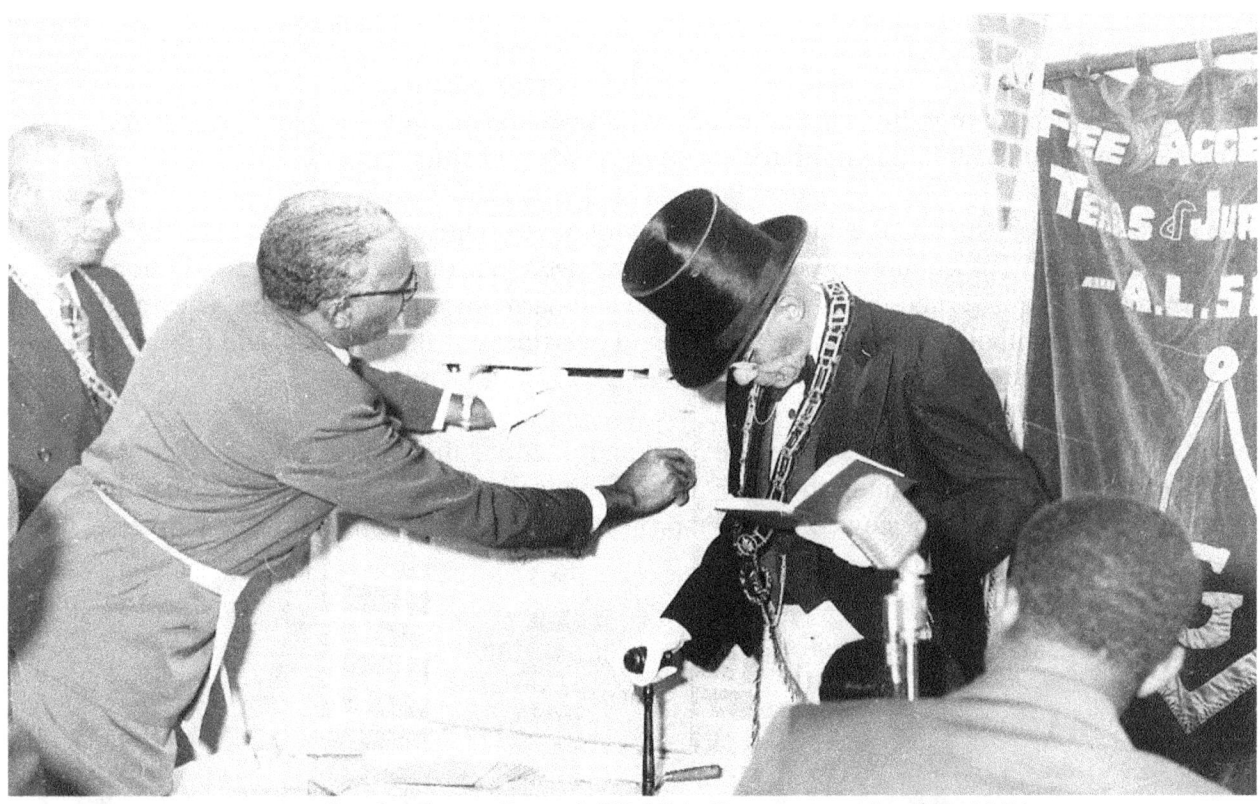
Bagby Street Branch YMCA Cornerstone Laying 1954

Bagby Street YMCA Cornerstone Laying Ceremony

Cornerstones and the ritualistic ceremonies are as old as the art of building. The ceremony began with the most ancient colonies and has been passed down through the civilizations of Egypt, Babylon, and Jerusalem.

The cornerstone laying ceremony performed for the Bagby Street Branch YMCA was the same service U.S. President George Washington used to lay the cornerstone in the nation's Capitol building in 1793. The nondenominational ceremony has religious overtones to *implore the divine blessing of God to protect the workmen from accident, and to bless those who conceived the erection of the edifice and its humanitarian purposes and all those who will enter through its doors.*

The dedication ceremony is the symbolic laying of the cornerstone which symbolically supports the entire building project including the actual physical actions to erect the building, the mental, spiritual, and metaphysical energies that have come together to cause the creation of the edifice. The Masons used ancient words to mimic the language of the operative masons, and they wore white aprons and white gloves as a badge of masonry to remind them of purity of life and conduct.

The Masonic officers conducting the ceremony symbolically square, level, and plumb the cornerstone, assuring that it is set correctly, that *the Craftsmen have done their duty*.

The three symbolic ancient building tools: a square, level and plumb were used by operative masons to assure the cornerstone was perfect and laid accurately, and they are symbolic guides for Masonry.

The square stands for morality: by the square, we square our actions. The level stands for equality of all people, and the plumb for rectitude of life and conduct.

The masons poured wine on the cornerstone to symbolize abundance and the need to refresh bodies and spirits. They poured oil to symbolize the need to soothe wounds and afflictions and further the spirit, peace, and joy of brotherly love and harmonious relationships. They also poured corn to symbolize nourishment, health and heartiness of the workers, and the sustaining of all who enter the building.

After the Grand Lodge officers squared, leveled and plumbed the cornerstone, the Grand Master *finished the work* by proclaiming the foundation stone *well formed, true and trusty* that these benefits and blessings be bestowed upon the project by the Great Architect of the Universe, God.

Dr. Chase W. Pemberton, Center about to present Silver Shovels to program participants- Grandmaster L.L. Lockhart, Gilbert Jackson, Reverend H.O. Scott, Maxey, O.W.L. Turner, Edward J. Mosher, Dr. E.B. Berry, Robert J. Maloney, and J.H. Jemison

THIRTY-SIXTH
ANNUAL MEETING
And
Building Campaign Kickoff

BAGBY BRANCH
YOUNG MENS CHRISTIAN ASSOCLATION
Houston and Harris County, Texas

Pilgrim Building Auditorium
January 21, 1955
7:30 P. M.

THE HOUSTON YOUNG MEN'S CHRISTIAN ASSOCIATION
BOARD OF DIRECTORS
OFFICERS

President	Edward J. Mosher.
Vice President	R. A. Marnsworth
Vice President	R. A. Childress
Vice President	Wendel D. Ley....
Recording Secretary	J. O. Webb
Treasurer	James E. Anderson
General Secretary	Robert J. Maloney
Associate General Secretary	W. A. Russell

BOARD OF MANAGEMENT

Chairman	Dr. E. B. Perry
Vice Chairman	J. H. Jemison
Vice Chairman	Arthur McCullough, Jr.
Recording Secretary	Theo Harris
Assistant Recording Secretary	Henry J. Bolding, Jr.
Treasurer	Judson W. Robinson

Dr. John E. Codwell	Dr. John W. Davis	Dr. John L. Brown
C.A. Dupree	P. E. Gallagher	Arthur M. Gaines, Jr.
Daniel Gay	W. L. D. Johnson, Jr.	Wm. S. Holland
W. P. Jordan	L. J. Mann	Dr. R. O'Hara Lanier
J. C. McDade	Emerson C. Norris	R. Moore
Dr. C. W. Pemberton	W. G. Strain	L. H. Spivey
Hobart T. Taylor	Archie Wells	H. M. Washington
James W. White	Eddie Young	James M. Calhoun
James R. Cunningham		

STAFF

Executive Secretary	Quentin R. Mease
Youth Work Secretary	Lawrence G. Sims
Physical Director	James F. Brooks
Community Program Secretary	Curtis Nicholson
Camp and Boys' Work Secretary	James A. Walls*
Assistant Boys' Work Secretary	Joseph D. Linton
Office Secretary	Bertha L. Johnson

* On Leave--Military Service

Chairman's Annual Message

1954 has been our finest year. We have realized a trinity of vital and significant achievements, namely: Groundbreaking for our New Building; Dedication of Camp Holden; and the impressive Cornerstone Ceremonies for our future *home*.

That They All May Be One are the meaningful words that are carved in the Cornerstone. Our organizational efforts during 1954 have carried out this altruistic concept in all areas of activity. Our board, staff, and volunteers continue to function cooperatively and effectively as One.

The intangible has now become a tangible reality-one of the most modern Y buildings in the world will shortly be ours. This fact alone will give impetus to the implementation of the four-fold program of spiritual, mental, physical, and social improvement for our membership.

The 1954 membership effort surpassed, numerically and financially, all previous endeavors. Our citizenry has clearly demonstrated their endorsement of the Y's program.

Camp Holden has continued to grow in facilities and popularity. Substantial improvements were made to capital structures as well as equipment. It has become a mecca for all races, colors, and creeds.

A consistently expanding recreational program has involved the participation of Y groups from other locations of our great city. The results of their relationships have been most encouraging.

World Services, the missionary program of the YMCA, again received wonderful support from our school clubs, sponsors, and principals. The expanded activities of the Youth Work Department is due in no Small measure to the fine cooperation received from our school friends.

This is the time for taking stock of our great enterprise. I commend this report to you for your very close perusal. It contains succinct information and data concerning the *State of the Association*. It presents a record of achievement of which we all may be proud.

E. B. Perry, M.D. Chairman Board of Management

Dr. J.L. Patton, Principal of Booker T. Washington High School, Dallas, Guest Speaker and Dr. W. Davis

Dr. E.B. Perry, Branch Chairman, Toastmaster addresses the dais and dinner audience

PROGRAM
Part 1
Dr. E. B. Perry, Toastmaster

The Invocation	The Reverend A. W. Harley, Pastor Mount Vernon Methodist Church
Dinner	
The Annual Report	Theo Harris, Secretary Board of Management
Report of Nominating Committee	J. C. McDade, Chairman
A Charge to New Members	Edward J. Mosher, President Houston and Harris County YMCA
Selections	Jack Yates High School Octette Mrs. Gloria Duke, Directress
Introduction of Guest Speaker	T. R. Chatham, Principal E.O. Smith Junior High School
Address	J. L. Patton, Principal Booker T. Washington High School Dallas, Texas
Recognitions	Robert Wilson, Chairman Awards Committee

YMCA SERVICE AWARD
1955

HERE is the truly Christian life, here is faith really working by love, when a man applies himself with joy and love to the works of that freest servitude in which he serve others voluntarily and for nought, himself abundantly satisfied in the fullness and riches of his own faith.
                                                                    Martin Luther

Jesse C. McDade

J. C. McDade has spent practically all of his adulthood in the service of the Young Men's Christian Association. His experience with the Army YMCA during World War I provided him with the conviction that the Association was a means through which he could express his basic concern about Christian training and leadership of youth. His contribution to that leadership through the years has been most constructive and inspiring.

He has been identified with Association work in Houston since the founding of the first branch in 1918, serving continuously as a board member and active layman until the present. A chairman of several important board committees during this time, he found his niche as chairman of the Boys' Work (now Youth Work) Department in which position he has remained for the past twenty-two years. A past vice chairman of the Board of Management, he was a faithful worker and leader in the 1939 and 1952 Building Fund Campaigns.

Arthur McCullough, Jr

Effective service cannot be measured in terms of years alone. Although a young man with less than ten year service on the Board of Management, Arthur McCullough, Jr. has compiled a record of achievement that compares most favorably with men with much longer connection and experience in the Movement. He has progressed rapidly in influence and position in Association circles in a comparatively short time.

He has been chairman of the Boys Membership Committee since 1948 annually leads in the production of boys' memberships for the branch. As general chairman of the 1953 and 1954 membership campaign, his leadership contributed greatly to the success of those drives and the rising of the branch membership to new heights. A member of the Building Program Committee since 1952, who was elected a vice president of the Board of Management in 1954.

W.L.D. Johnson, Jr., presents Meritorious Service Plaque to J.C. McDade, board member, for distinguished service to the branch. The YMCA Service Award observed at the ceremony at the Thirty-Sixth Annual Meeting and Building Campaign Kickoff 1955

W.L.D. Johnson, Jr., Arthur McCullough, J.C. McDade, and Mrs. E.B. Perry

Qualifications For
The YMCA Service Award

1. Long and faithful attention to responsibilities in the Young Men's Christian Association--local, area, or National.
2. Outstanding and exceptional leadership and contribution to the progress of the Association Movement.
3. Regular and consistent attendance at meetings of a Council, Board, or Committees of which he is a Member.
4. Personal exemplification of the Christian purposes and ideals of the Young Men's Christian Association.

Committee
Harold Clark   A. L. Patterson
Robert Wilson, Chairman

W.L.D. Johnson, Jr., presents Meritorious Service Plaque to Arthur McCullough, Jr, board member, for distinguished service to the branch. The YMCA Service Award observed at the ceremony at the Thirty-Sixth Annual Meeting and Building Campaign Kickoff 1955

Edward J. Mosher, President of Houston YMCA addressing the dinner audience at the 1955 Building Campaign Kickoff

Building Campaign Kickoff 1955

Arthur Harding YMCA National Council addresses dinner audience at Building Campaign Kickoff 1955

PROGRAM
Part II

BUILDING CAMPAIGN KICKOFF

Campaign Statement   Robert J. Maloney, General Secretary
                                                                            Houston And Harris (County YMCA

Introductions   Dr. C.W. Pemberton, Chairman
                                                                                       Citizen Sponsors Committee

Presentation of Campaign Leaders   Dr. John W. Davis, Chairman
                                                                                                Special Gifts Committee

                                                                                               Judson W. Robinson, Chairman
                                                                                                       Section I

                                                                           William S. Holland, Chairman
                                                                                                    Section II

Instructions to Workers   Arthur W. Hardy
                                                                                                        Campaign Director

Benediction

A NEW YEAR CHALLENGE

Our New YMCA Building will be an eventuation within the next few months. Our Members, Friends, Board of Management, Staff, Metropolitan Board and General Secretary are all anxiously awaiting the data when that long held dream-of this ultra-modern, beautiful and functional building- becomes a reality as soon as possible, The Building Program Committee, composed of J.H. Jemison, Chairman; C.A. Dupree, Hobart T. Taylor, Dr. E.B. Perry, Judson R. Robinson, Sr. and Arthur McCullough, Jr. have spent the past three years in study, review, and deliberation around the New building plans. These Gentlemen are justly proud of the part they have played in the conception and construction of the fine YMCA plant now nearing completion at Wheeler and Sampson.

They desire no praise for the thousands of hours of hard work and thinking that have gone into the creation of this fine new edifice. But they do ask that you -Citizen of Houston- give your unstinting support to the *Let's Finish the Job Building Campaign* that opens tonight.

Some Features of the New Building

Spacious lounge for youth and adults
Power equipped craft shop Gymnasium
66x94 All Purpose
Grill and All Purpose Kitchen
Chapel And Vestry
68 Residence Rooms All Single
Beautiful Patio and Dinning Terrace
5Acre Site-Large 0utdoor Game Area
Ample Parking Area for 200 cars
Installation for future Air-conditioning

Community Group Auditorium (250 per person seating capacity}
Club rooms for youth and adults
Natatorium-25x60 swimming pool
Space for additional club rooms and Men's Health Club
Locker Rooms and Showers for boys and girls, men and women
Automatic High Speed Elevator
Provision for future expansion

BAGBY BRANCH ACTIVITIES
Statistical Summary

GROUP ACTIVITIES	Enrollment	No. of Groups	Sessions	Attendance
Clubs	895	61	452	15,793
Classes	23	3	22	746
Teams	158	15	78	18,993
Spec. Int. Groups	60	1	15	189
Councils and Committees	130	7	21	292
Other	280	4	12	320
GROUPS WITHOUT DEFINITE				
Special Events		41	67	13,313
Informal Groups		13	43	4,784

Individual Services
Personal Interview — 955
Game Room Usage — 1,927

OUTSIDE GROUPS USING YMCA FACILITIES	Number	Attendance
	75	5,490

Sources of Income

Memberships	$ 8,440.09
Program Services	6,881.60
United Fund	26,150.00
Total Income	$41,471.89

Expenses

Administration	$26,153.56
Programs	11,694.57
Building and Maintenance	3,617.41
Total Expenditures	$41,365.69
Balance at End of Year	$ 106.15

ANNUAL MEETING COMMITTEE

W. L. D. Johnson, Jr., Chairman	Harold Clark
Mrs. Anna Dupree	Arthur M. Gaines, Jr.
Rev. A. W. Harley	Mrs. Martha McAfee
Dr. Fred D. Parrott	Andrew Patterson
James F. Ragin	Mrs. Jessie Robertson
Dr. James T. Sprott	Robert Wilson

Building Program Radiothon 1955
Vernon Chambers left Radio Station KCOH Program Director and A.E. Warner Director of the successful Radiothon for the Building Campaign on February 12, 1955.

Left to right: L.H. Spivey, A.E. Warner, L.W. Dickerson, Owner of Club Matinee

Building Campaign Captains and Workers
Left to right: Dr. John W. Davis, Dr. E.B. Perry, Robert Taylor, Henry J. Bolding, and Joe B. Jones

William C. Craver former Branch Executive raises the arm of Henry Jerome Bolding, Jr., Top Division Leader of the 1955 Drive

Lamar Fleming, Jr. South Central YMCA Dedication Ceremony April 24, 1955

South Central YMCA Dedication Ceremony and Open House

The fashionable, modernistic new million dollar South Central YMCA Building was open to the public for the first time with a ribbon cutting ceremony following the dedication program on Sunday afternoon, April 24, before an estimated 5,000 persons. The dedication was presided over by Edward J. Mosher, President of the Metropolitan YMCA Board of Directors. Dr. E.B. Perry, Chairman of the Board of Management of the South Central YMCA, was Master of Ceremonies for the Dedication Program and Clarence Arnold Dupree, Houston Realtor and Investment Banker, was Chairman of the Arrangements Committee for the program and open house. Dowdal H. Davis, General Manager of the Kansas City Call, was the principal speaker. He called for *the development of a philosophy of ideals to sustain the confidence of other nations in our interpretation of a democratic way of life. Far too long have we preached democracy and practiced the opposite.*

Brief presentations were made by Dr. R. O'Hara Lanier, President of Texas Southern University; Robert W. Kneebone, Vice President of the United Fund of Houston and Harris County; Dr. John W. Davis, local Dentist, Lamar Fleming, Jr. Chairman of the Board of Directors, Anderson, the world's largest cotton brokers, Clayton Company, and Hobart Taylor, Transportation Executive. Robert J. Maloney, General Secretary of the Houston YMCA, made an interpretative statement.

South Central YMCA Dedication Ceremony April 24, 1955

Tom Tellepsen, Chairman of the Architectural Advisory Committee, turned over the keys to Robert A. Childers, Vice President of the Metropolitan YMCA Board, who, in turn gave them to J.H. Jemison, Chairman of the Building Committee of the South Central YMCA.

To Lamar Fleming Jr. went the honor of cutting the ribbon and first to enter the new structure. Having personally given $350,000 to the building program and obtaining an additional $300,000 from the MD Anderson Foundation. Mr. Fleming was the principal benefactor for the new Y facility.

South Central YMCA Ribbon Cutting Ceremony
Quentin R. Mease, J.H. Jemison, Dr. Charles Whittaker Pemberton April 24, 1955

Lobby of South Central YMCA 1955

South Central YMCA Snack Bar Bennie L. White, Joe Williams, Archie Duncan, Joe B. Jones and Pleas Smith

1955 South Central YMCA Century Chart

South Central YMCA Beautiful Chapel

Services in Chapel

86

South Central YMCA Indoor Pool

87

Pleas Smith and Joe Williams first occupants of South Central YMCA Elevator

South Central YMCA Residence

References

25th Century Club Annual Meeting. Thursday, May 18, 1972. A Salute to Our Century Clubbers.

Bagby Street YMCA 1951 Annual Program.

Bagby Street YMCA 1954 Annual Program.

Bagby Street YMCA 1955 Annual Program.

Dr. Charles Jackson, c. 1920s (Courtesy of Riverside General Hospital and Drs. Levi V. and Eula Perry).

Dr. Rupert O. Roett, c.1918 (Printed in Houston Informer, courtesy of Riverside General Hospital and Drs. Levi V. and Eula Perry).

Greater Houston Black Chamber Cornerstone at 2808 Wheeler Street.

Jackson, Andrew Webster. 1938. A Sure Foundation & A Sketch of Negro Life in Texas.

Joel Weintraub transcriber from 1931-32 City Directory and 1940 Street Directory.

Mease, Quentin R. 2001. On Equal Footing. Eakin Press.

Prairie View A&M University History and Traditions. Retrieved on July 15, 2018 from www.pvamu.edu.

RGH Riverside General Hospital History http://riversidegeneralhospital.org.

Scott Emmett J. 1919. The American Negro in the World War. Chapter XXVIII. Chicago Homewood Press.

The Gregory School. 2019. http://www.thegregoryschool.org/library.html.

The Houston Informer (Houston, Texas) Saturday, July 17, 1920.

The Houston Informer (Houston, Texas) Saturday, November 27, 1920.

The Houston Informer (Houston, Texas) Vol 2, No. 52, Ed.1 Saturday, May 14, 1921 page:1of 8. The

Houston Informer (Houston, Texas) Vol 4, No. 39, Ed. 1 Saturday, February 17, 1923 page:1 of 8.

The Houston Informer (Houston, Texas) Vol 4, No. 48, Ed. 1 Saturday, April 21, 1923 page:1 of 10.

The Houston Informer (Houston, Texas) Vol 5, No. 21, Ed. 1 Saturday, October 13, 1923 page:5 of 8.

The Houston Informer (Houston, Texas) Vol 5, No. 39, Ed. 1 Saturday, February 16, 1924 page:1 of 8.

The Houston Informer (Houston, Texas). January 1-December 31, 1947-1949.

The Houston Informer (Houston, Texas), January 1-December 31, 1948-1950.

The Pilgrim Building Alumni Reunion Reception Program. November 25, 1995.

The Pittsburgh Courier Pittsburgh, Pennsylvania. Saturday, June 16, 1928 page 14.

The Pittsburgh Courier Pittsburgh, Pennsylvania. Saturday, February 18, 1939 page 22.

The Pittsburgh Courier Pittsburgh, Pennsylvania. Saturday, June3, 1939 page 22.

The Pittsburgh Courier Pittsburgh, Pennsylvania. Saturday, December 11, 1943 page 13.

The Pittsburgh Courier Pittsburgh, Pennsylvania. Saturday, February 12, 1944 page 12.

The Pittsburgh Courier Pittsburgh, Pennsylvania. Saturday, January 4, 1947 page 14.

The Pittsburgh Courier Pittsburgh, Pennsylvania. Saturday, January 25, 1947 page 14.

The Pittsburgh Courier Pittsburgh, Pennsylvania. Saturday, February 15, 1947 page 18.

The Pittsburgh Courier Pittsburgh, Pennsylvania. Saturday, March 1, 1947 page 14.

The Pittsburgh Courier Pittsburgh, Pennsylvania. Saturday, June12, 1948 page 12.

The Pittsburgh Courier Pittsburgh, Pennsylvania. Saturday, August 13, 1949 page 20.

The Pittsburgh Courier Pittsburgh, Pennsylvania. Saturday, June12, 1951 page 12.

The Pittsburgh Courier Pittsburgh, Pennsylvania. Saturday, March 29, 1952 page 18.

The Red Book of Houston (Houston: Sontex Publishing Company, circa 1915) pages 22, 24, 72, 151.

Nichols, Gary. 2011. YMCA of Greater Houston Archives #30.

www.ingramcontent.com/pod-product-compliance
Lightning Source LLC
Chambersburg PA
CBHW080415170426
43194CB00015B/2820